Library Learning Information

Idea Store® Chrisp Street
1 Vesey Path
East India Dock Road
London   E14 6BT

020 7364 4332
www.ideastore.co.uk

Created and managed by
Tower Hamlets Council

To Tara Taylor

With thanks to David and Charlotte Hodes
and also to Celia, Emily, Esme, Jasmine and Rosa

Midnight Feast Magic copyright © Frances Lincoln Limited 2008
Text copyright © Rosalind Peters and Polly Peters 2008
Illustrations copyright © Kate Pankhurst 2008
Photographs copyright © Clive Boursnall 2008
Designed by Rachel Hamdi/Holly Fulbrook

First published in Great Britain in 2008 and the USA in 2009 by
Frances Lincoln Children's Books,
4 Torriano Mews, Torriano Avenue, London NW5 2RZ
www.franceslincoln.com

British Library Cataloguing in Publication Data available on request

ISBN: 978-1-84507-783-9

Printed in China

1 3 5 7 9 8 6 4 2

Midnight Feast Magic

Illustrated by
KATE PANKHURST

Photography by
CLIVE BOURSNALL

**Rosalind Peters
and Polly Peters**

F

FRANCES LINCOLN
CHILDREN'S BOOKS

Contents

Ultimate sleepover fun and feasting

Welcome to MIDNIGHT FEAST MAGIC. I have travelled from afar (well, Shropshire actually) to share my book of ravishing recipes for the perfect sleepover and awesome activities for staying up late.

I love everything about sleepovers: the planning, the preparation, the NOT sleeping! I'm not sure how many of these recipes actually got eaten at midnight – it's just too long to wait with treats that look and smell as good as these do.

Forget filling up a supermarket trolley with lots of over-priced, ready-made snacks. The best sleepover feasts are the ones you make yourselves. Trust me and remember the saying: "You are what you eat." That makes me nuts... and my friends, bananas!

Rosalind Peters

Planning your scrumptious sleepover

First things first: all the recipes are simple and fairly easy. Each one has been tried and tested and if I can do it, then believe me, anyone can.

The chapters feature different parts of a feast. Use the book like a pick 'n' mix depending on whether you just want one or two snacks, a collection of crazy cocktails or a sumptuous feasting fest.

Decide which parts of your menu you are going to make before your guests arrive. (Anything in the Freezer Frenzy section for definite, otherwise it will be "Unfrozen and Frantic!") For me though, the fun starts with everyone getting their hands sticky. Share the making, share the eating!

Shopping

Make a shopping list for any ingredients you don't already have.

For any last-minute, unplanned, sleepover snacking, don't despair! There's a section called "Cupboard's bare" using ingredients you might already have at home.

To weigh or not to weigh?

How much measuring do you need to do? Some recipes do need precise quantities (like pretzels, or anything containing flour). However, others are more open to imagination. Fruit smoothies for example can be whizzed up with a huge range of fruit and juice combinations and you can slosh it all in without too much worry about measuring jugs.

Vegetarian, vegan and wheat free

V   Recipes suitable for vegetarians are marked with a 'v'.

☀   Recipes suitable for vegans are marked with a star.

♥   Recipes suitable for anyone with a wheat allergy are marked with a heart.

Remember that some recipes can be vegan or allergy-friendly by substituting some of the ingredients. Feel free to experiment!

Best use of adults

Adults can be very useful helpers but they need proper training!

They are allowed to help with important stuff, like showing you how to safely operate the oven, grill and cooker hob or how to use oven gloves properly to avoid burning your fingers when taking things out of the oven. They are also really useful for demonstrating methods such as safest use of knives or telling you just how exactly the blender works and where to find the whizzy attachments. However, they are absolutely NOT allowed to do anything for you that you could reasonably manage yourself AND THIS INCLUDES CLEARING UP AFTERWARDS!

If you can prove that you are responsible enough to not only prepare your own feasting treats but to leave the kitchen clean and tidy, it is MUCH more likely that you'll be allowed to do it again! See – clever, huh?

In fact, keeping the adults happy is rule number one for the successful sleepover. So, get messy – but tidy up afterwards; have fun, be noisy, but plan some really quiet activities for when you're told to "hush in there". Believe me, it's worth it in the long run.

Awesome activities

No sleepover is complete without awesome activities to keep the fun flowing. Keeping a camera on hand is a really smart way of catching immortal moments. You could make a scrapbook of the sleepover afterwards, especially for a big occasion like a birthday. Another great way to create a keepsake is to use a roll of plain wallpaper to tape down onto the table. Get everyone to decorate and sign and date it to make a one-off tablecloth.

What are you waiting for? Go ahead – tantalize those taste buds...

Essential Equipment

Baking tins and trays
Blender or food processor
chopping board
Cocktail umbrellas
Cookie-cutter
Colander
Cup-cake cases
Grater
Jelly moulds
Serving jug
frying pan
Saucepans of assorted sizes
Rolling pin
Measuring jugs
Straws
Ice-cream scoop
Whisk
Wooden spoon

delicious drinks

Dazzlingly delightful fruity flavours, smoothies and crazy cocktail concoctions.

Recipes:
❀ Smoothies ❀ Real lemonade ❀ Jelly juice ❀ Pineapple and strawberry ice slushies
❀ Izzy, whizzy, tangy, fizzy pzzazzz ❀ Milkshakes to remember ❀ Hot chocolate

Smoothies V ♥

Just because something is healthy doesn't mean it can't be delicious too. These smoothies are like paradise in a glass.

Ingredients

- Fruit of your choice (see suggestions below)
- Yoghurt (plain Greek style, live yoghurt or low fat fruit yoghurt)
- Fruit juice (for if your smoothie is more gloopy than smooth)

What you do

The basic technique is the same for all smoothies and is stunningly simple.

1. Prepare fruit by washing/peeling/chopping.

2. Place it all in a blender and whizz until all the fruit has been reduced to a pulp. If adding yoghurt or juice, add along with the fruit before blending.

That's it! Now try your hand at advanced smoothies...

Kiwi Taste Buds

Four kiwi fruits, half a carton of strawberries, two large apples, and two large oranges: one squeezed and one peeled and chopped. You do need to chop the apple into smallish chunks too. Serve with a thin slice of kiwi and half a strawberry sitting on top.

Very Berry

I tend to use the quantities of fruit we actually have, rather than measuring specifically. This smoothie can mix any number of beautiful berries. Try raspberries, blackberries, blueberries, strawberries, two tablespoons of Greek yoghurt, one dessertspoon of runny honey and half to one cup of either cranberry, pomegranate or apple juice.

Raspberry Squish

One cup of raspberry yoghurt, one cup frozen raspberries, one cup of milk, two soft pears (peeled, cored and chopped).

Oh So Peachy

Three peaches or nectarines, one large banana, one cup of frozen or fresh raspberries and the juice of two large oranges (or a good slosh of orange juice from a carton).

The Apple's Gone Bananas!

One cup of orange juice, two bananas, two apples, half a cup of plain yoghurt.

Strawberry, Pineapple Spill

One tin of chopped pineapple including juice, two bananas and about twenty strawberries.

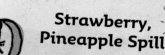

11

Truth or Dare?

Real lemonade is perfect to drink while playing truth or dare: it has the sweetness of truth with the sharpness of a dare. Are you telling the truth?

To play truth or dare you need two or more people. You will take it in turns to answer either a truth or a dare or you can spin a bottle. The person it points to when it stops is the next player. Choose who asks the questions or take it in turns. To decide on either a truth or dare, the player can throw a dice (1-3 is a truth question, 4-6 is a dare) or flip a coin. Here are a few ideas to start you off.

Dare:

- Practise a sloppy kiss against the back of your hand
- Sing 'humpty dumpty' as though it is the saddest story you have ever heard.
- Stand on one leg and repeat, "I am the quick-witted queen of England" ten times without falling over.
- Pick up a pencil with your toes and draw a face.

When answering a truth question, the other players must decide if you're actually telling the truth.

Truth:

- What's your worst habit?
- If you were stranded on a desert island, what three things would you take with you?
- Have you ever had a crush on a famous actor or popstar?
- What has been your most embarrassing moment?
- If you could only rescue one thing from your bedroom, what would it be?

Real Lemonade ∨ ☀ ♥

This is the real deal – not fizzy, but deliciously sour and sweet at the same time. You have NOT tasted lemonade until you've tried this.

Ingredients

- 2 Lemons
- Water (approx 3 cups)
- Caster (fine granule) sugar
- Ice cubes

What you do

1. Cut the lemons in half and squeeze out all the juice with a lemon squeezer.

2. Pour all the juice into a jug and then dilute it with water.

3. Add sugar until it is sweet enough for your taste. I use about 5 teaspoons. Stir really fast until all the sugar has dissolved.

4. Add the ice cubes and pour it into tall glasses.

5. Pop in straws and an extra slice of lemon for decoration. *Mmmmmmm!*

Why did the two lemons cross the road? Because they wanted to play squash!

Jelly juice ♥

Is it a drink? Is it a pudding? No, it's a jelly (jello) drink! Drink the top section and scoop out the bottom with a spoon! If you want to be really adventurous, you can even try layering two different colours of jelly to make stripy jelly juice!

I like using vegetarian jelly but you can also use standard jelly as long as none of your guests are vegetarian.

Ingredients

- Packet(s) of jelly (jello), flavour of your choice
- Fruit juice (any flavour)
- Lemon or orange for squeezing (optional)
- Chopped fruit (optional)

What you do

1. Make up the jelly (jello) according to the instructions on the packet, in a measuring jug. If I'm making lemon jelly I always squeeze a lemon in before topping up with boiling water (or an orange for orange jelly and sometimes, frozen raspberries into raspberry jelly). It makes it taste MUCH more tangy and fruity.

2. Pour the jelly mix into glasses, up to about a third full. Leave to set. (If you want to make stripy jelly, you will need to pour in to a depth of about 2cm (3/4 inch), leave to set and then repeat with a different flavour and colour of jelly.)

3. When solid, pour the fruit juice over. Add chopped fruit and ice cubes or juice cubes if you like. Half and half: drink first and then dive into the jelly.

13

Pineapple and strawberry ice slushies V ☀ ♥

This one is definitely one of my all time favourites, an easy concoction that I make again and again and again. I'm already reaching for the cocktail umbrellas...

The great thing about this sort of recipe is that you don't have to measure accurately – you can do it by taste.

Ingredients
- Strawberries (1 small carton or more!)
- Pineapple juice (4 cups)
- Pineapple chunks – either 1 small tin or half a small pineapple, chopped CAREFULLY.

What you do

1. A few hours beforehand, pour some of the pineapple juice into an ice-cube tray and leave to freeze.

2. When frozen put the pineapple ice-cubes into a blender and add half a cup of juice for each person.

3. Chop all the strawberries and put in the blender.

4. Add the pineapple chunks. Then put the lid on the blender. *(This may sound blindingly obvious but believe me, I know what I'm talking about! Oops, hello kitchen makeover.)*

5. Whizz the contents until slushy.

6. Pour the slushies into glasses. Add straws and cocktail umbrellas. Carry carefully to your room. *Slurp!*

Totally Top Tip
Save a few chopped strawberries to drop into your scrumptious slush-fest. Or use thin slices to decorate the edge of the glasses.

Strawberry and Oat Scrub

If you manage not to scoff all the strawberries, and you also have some plain yoghurt and some porridge oats, then you could try making this brilliant face scrub.

Ingredients

• A handful of strawberries • 2 tablespoons of plain yoghurt • 50g (2oz) of oats

What you do

1. De-stalk the strawberries and mash them with a fork. Mix together with the yoghurt.
2. Now add the oats and stir thoroughly until it's pink and gloopy.
3. Tie back your hair or use a hairband. Apply the face pack, rubbing it in a circular motion.
4. Leave it on for 5-10 minutes. Make faces at each other and play the "who can keep a straight face for longest, without laughing" game.
5. Remove with tissues first, then rinse off with warm water. Pat dry carefully with a towel.

It will leave your skin super-soft.

! Be careful not to apply next to your eyes.

Izzy whizzy, tangy, fizzy pzzazzz

This is my favourite drink name. It sounds just like one of those fancy fruit cocktails you find on a menu. It's simply a fizzy version of orange and lemonade, but it's wearing its best outfit and it sounds jolly spiffing, wouldn't you say darling?

Ingredients

• Lemons
• Oranges
• Fizzy, carbonated water
• Caster (fine granule) sugar

What you do

1. Allow one orange and half a lemon per person. Squeeze and pour into a glass.
2. Stir in one to two teaspoons of sugar per glass.
3. Top up with the fizzy water.
4. When drinking, don't let the bubbles go up your nose. Whatever is up your nostrils, let it stay there!

Totally Top Tip

Before you pour in the juice or fizz, dip the rim of each glass into water, then dip into a saucer of sugar for a sweetly frosted edging.

Milkshakes to remember ♥ ♥

Like the smoothies, milkshakes can be created according to what you have available. The secret treat tip is to float a scoop of ice-cream on the top.

The original milkshakes were shaken energetically in a large, metal jar.

You can still do this, using a wide-necked bottle, or use a blender or whisk.

Ingredients

- Milk (try variations with either soya or rice milk to avoid dairy products)
- Ice-cream (dairy or soya)
- Fruit/chocolate, according to taste

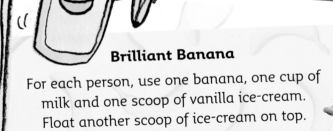

Cheeky Chocolicious

For each person, add one cup of milk and one scoop of chocolate ice-cream plus two squares of melted, dark chocolate. Whizzy, whizzy, let's get busy: whisk and shake. Grate more chocolate over the top.

Raspberry Choco-Ripple

Add raspberries to the above recipe for an unusual twist.

Brilliant Banana

For each person, use one banana, one cup of milk and one scoop of vanilla ice-cream. Float another scoop of ice-cream on top.

Raspberry Rascal

For each person, place one glass of milk, one scoop (or large spoon) of ice-cream and a handful of fruit into a blender or jug. Combine fruit flavours if you want: banana with raspberry or strawberry is a great mix. Either whizz in the blender or use a hand mixer to mix and to froth it up in a large jug.

Hot chocolate

This may be a well known and ages-old recipe but it is still one of my top comfort drinks, especially with marshmallows, whipped cream and grated chocolate.

Knock, knock
Who's there?
Ice-cream
Ice-cream who?
Ice-cream if you throw cold milk over me!

Ingredients

- Milk
- Hot chocolate powder
- Whipped cream or squirty cream
- Marshmallows

What you do

1. Measure out the required number of mugs of milk then heat, either in a jug in the microwave or in a small saucepan on the cooker hotplate.

2. Add chocolate powder for the number of mugs being made and stir very fast so it goes frothy on top.

3. Pour into mugs and float three or four marshmallows per mug before spooning over whipped cream (or artfully squirting cream).

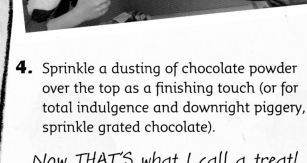

4. Sprinkle a dusting of chocolate powder over the top as a finishing touch (or for total indulgence and downright piggery, sprinkle grated chocolate).

Now THAT'S what I call a treat!

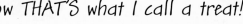

delightful dips

Perfectly perfect, suitably savoury and scrumptiously scrummy. Dip, dunk and dollop. Dive in and devour. Delicious!

Recipes:

- Tahini runny dip • Tzatziki • Hungry for houmous • Saucy salsa • Great guacamole

Tahini runny dip V ✳ ♥

This is particularly tasty with falafels (see page 35) but is just as good with crunchy things dunked in it. I also love this dribbled over a bowl of grated carrot (as an alternative to coleslaw for my vegan friend who doesn't eat mayonnaise).

Ingredients

- ¹/₂ cup of tahini
- 2 cloves of garlic
- ¹/₄ cup of lemon juice
- 2 tablespoons of olive oil
- ¹/₄ teaspoon of salt
- chopped parsley to sprinkle over when ready (optional)

What you do

1. Whizz the garlic, tahini and salt with a blender or processor. Empty into a bowl.

2. Stir in the oil and lemon juice until it's well mixed. Stirring gives it the right sort of runny consistency.

3. A scattering of chopped parsley over the top isn't vital but it does look nice and goes well with the garlic flavour.

Tzatziki V ♥

I love saying this word (pronounced *Zat-zee-kee*). It may sound like an alien race, featuring any time soon in *Dr Who*, but, in fact this yoghurty dip owes its great-sounding name to its Greek and Turkish origins. There are as many variations in making this dish as there are people to eat it. It's up to you and your taste buds (or make that your tasting buddies, seeing as you'll probably be making this with your friends).

Ingredients

- Plain yoghurt (preferably strained yoghurt or thick, Greek yoghurt. Traditionally, it is made with sheep's yoghurt.)
- ¹/₂ a cucumber
- ¹/₂–1 clove of crushed garlic
- 1 dessertspoon of white vinegar
- up to 1 tablespoon of olive oil
- chopped fresh parsley or chopped fresh mint

What you do

1. Peel and finely chop the cucumber. Put it in a bowl and pour over the yoghurt.

2. Stir in all the other ingredients you are adding. That's it! Ready to dive in.

Hungry for houmous V ♥

There are so many possible ways to eat this Middle Eastern chickpea smoothie: dip crunchy things into it, pile it into pitta bread, spread it in a sandwich or on a cracker or serve with Fluffy Falafels (see page 35).

Ingredients

- I can of chickpeas (drain out the liquid into a cup)
- I-2 cloves of crushed garlic
- I tablespoon of tahini (or 2 tablespoons of plain yoghurt)
- 3-5 tablespoons of lemon juice
- 2 tablespoons of olive oil
- 1/2 teaspoon of salt
- pinch of ground cumin (optional)
- a pinch of cayenne pepper to sprinkle on the top when it's ready to serve (optional)
- pine nuts to stir in when ready to serve (optional)

What you do

1. Give all the ingredients a whirl in the blender and serve.
2. A tiny pinch of sprinkled cayenne pepper looks pretty AND gives it a bit of bite. You could also stir in a handful of pine nuts or sprinkle them over the top.

How can you find celery in the fridge? Stalk it!

Saucy salsa V ☀ ♥

I am in *luurve* with this Mexican dip. It positively tap-dances on the taste buds. In fact it tangos tangfastically. And it's super-de-dooperly simple to throw together too.

Ingredients

- I tin of chopped tomatoes (or 4 large, fresh tomatoes, chopped)
- I or 2 cloves of crushed garlic
- 1/2 a small onion, chopped
- 1/4 teaspoon of salt
- I tablespoon of olive oil
- juice of 1/2 a lime (or 1/2 small lemon)
- a pinch of dried oregano
- The flesh of I small jalapeno pepper, chopped (this is where the heat will come from, so you may want to begin with 1/2 or 1/4 of the pepper while you test how hot you like it)

! Wash your hands with soap after handling the pepper and never touch your eyes or nose until those hands are well scrubbed. The heat of the jalapeno will sting if you do!

What you do

1. Put all ingredients together. Whizz with either a blender or a food processor until there are no lumpy bits left.
2. Pour into a bowl or store in the fridge in a lidded jar until you're ready.

Great guacamole V ♥

This Mexican dish was first made in the age of the Aztecs of South America.

It goes very well with salsa, tastes great with tortilla corn chips and is also traditionally served in a taco (see page 37). This recipe is for the basic dip but you can spice it up by adding tomato, coriander, jalapeno pepper and onion.

What you do

1. Whizz all the ingredients together (or you can mash and bash with a strong fork).
2. Eat and enjoy!

Ingredients

- 2 ripe avocados (sliced in half and scraped out of their skin with a spoon)
- 2 cloves of crushed garlic
- 3 tablespoons of lime juice (you could use lemon juice but lime tastes best)
- ½ teaspoon of salt
- 1 tablespoon of plain yoghurt or crème fraiche (optional)

Awful Alphabet Anecdotes

Can you tell a story using the letters of the alphabet to begin each successive word? Does it make sense? Is it seriously silly? How far can you get through the alphabet without stopping? Either try going round in a circle, with each person adding the next word, OR try one at a time to see who can get more than halfway through the alphabet.

Anna
begins
cracking
dangerous
eggs
for
garnishing
her
irritating
jelly
Kitten...

21

savoury snacks

Bite-sized bits for savouring the moment. Perfect for early evening before you gorge yourself with sweet treats.

Recipes:

✿ We're crackers! Funky faces ✿ Toasted nuts and seeds ✿ Popcorn ✿ Perfect pink pretzels
✿ Sausage sleeping bags ✿ Layer sandwiches ✿ Roly poly sandwiches

We're Crackers!
Funky Faces V

These are really good fun to create together. You can even turn it into a competition with prizes for the best cracker faces and a photo gallery of each finished face.

Ingredients

- Large square or round crackers
- Butter or margarine
- Soft cheese or paté or savoury spread
- Various salad toppings for decorating such as olives, cress, chives, shredded lettuce, thin strips of red pepper, slices of cucumber, slices of radish and grated cheese

Spread each cracker with butter/margarine and anything else spreadable on top. (The butter stops the cracker going soggy by the way). Then use this as a sticky base for arranging salad toppings into the shape of funny, funky faces.

Let your imaginations run riot! In fact, if you use a mix of round and square crackers you can create a whole cracker person and dress it with salad!

Designer Party Bag
You will need:

- Large pieces of strong paper (a roll of wallpaper is ideal)
- Any of the following: old magazines or used wrapping paper, coloured paper, ribbon/thick string/raffia, felt tip pens, crayons/pastels, marker pens, sequins, any small, flat objects that could be glued on, glue, scissors, sticky tape and a stapler.

First, make your bag. You simply fold a long piece of paper in half and seal down the two sides.

Make handles from ribbon or string or folded paper strips. Decorate! Draw your own pattern, logo or slogan, or add paper ruffles inside and out. You can add pockets too. Sign and date your creation. Who knows? It may be a collector's item some day!

chive eyelashes

olive eyes

half radish smiles

red pepper bow tie

cress or shredded lettuce or grated cheese hair

cucumber earrings

red pepper smiles

Toasted nuts and seeds

These are brilliant to nibble on, delicious, full of protein and just as yummy as crisps. Who said that healthy things don't taste great? They are plain wrong, wrong, WRONG.

I usually use almonds, broken cashew nuts, hazelnuts, sunflower seeds or pumpkin seeds. You can use any one of these on its own or you can mix together any combination, according to what you have. You can toast as much or as little as you want.

Ingredients

- Nuts or seeds (or a mixture of both)
- Spices (if making spicy nuts)

What you do

For plain, toasted nuts

1. Shake the nuts and/or seeds over a baking tray. You need a single layer of nuts/seeds so that everything is spread out evenly.

2. Place under the grill and turn the grill to a high heat. You will need to stand watch over this now to make sure you don't over-toast the nuts.

3. Check the nuts/seeds every minute. What you are looking for is a light browning of the outside of the nut. If you're using almonds or seeds, the skins will also have begun to split.

4. Using a pair of oven gloves, shake the tin from side to side. Any nuts that look as though they are turning a darker brown should be flipped over with a teaspoon.

5. Remove from grill as soon as the nuts/seeds are mostly lightly toasted on both sides. If in doubt, it is better to under toast than to overdo it.

Tip into a bowl and allow to cool before munching.

For spicy nuts

1. Place a non-stick frying pan over a high heat.

2. Add either one teaspoon of mixed spices or, $1/4$-$1/2$ a teaspoon of ground cumin plus $1/4$-$1/2$ a teaspoon of ground coriander and a $1/4$ teaspoon of turmeric.

3. Stir with a wooden spoon for one minute, then turn the hob down to medium heat and add about 250g (8oz) of mixed nuts and seeds.

4. Stir well to get the spices evenly mixed. Make sure you are using a wooden or heat-proof spoon. If you use a metal spoon, it will scratch and spoil your non-stick pan.

5. Keep stirring until you hear the nuts beginning to pop their skins and until there is a light, toasty browning of the mix.

6. Empty into a serving bowl and allow to cool. You can sprinkle over a pinch of salt at this point, but I prefer them unsalted.

For savoury sunflower seeds

1. Place a non-stick frying pan over a high heat.

2. Add 250g (8oz) of sunflower seeds and one dessert spoon of soy sauce. Stir to mix together well.

3. Keep stirring with the pan on a high heat for about three minutes, then turn down to a medium heat.

4. When the sunflower seeds begin to pop their skins, stir for one more minute then remove from heat and serve when cool. Yumtious!

Popcorn V ♥

Whoever told us we needed a popcorn-maker to make popcorn had something to sell! Home-made popcorn tastes SO much nicer than packet AND you get to eat it warm, with just the right amount of flavouring.

Ingredients

• 2 tablespoons of popping corn
• 1 tablespoon of sunflower oil
• Butter • Salt

! DON'T use the best saucepan in the kitchen! Popcorn can very occasionally leave dark brown marks in the bottom of a pan that take AGES to scrub off!

What you do

1. Use a saucepan with a tightly-fitting lid. Place it on a high heat and add a tablespoon of sunflower oil. Allow it to heat up for a minute without the lid.

2. Pour in the popcorn and stir with a wooden or heatproof spoon to make sure that the corn is well coated with oil.

3. Place the lid on the pan and keep it on a high heat for two minutes, occasionally shaking it from side to side to help prevent sticking. (If it sticks, it can burn and leave brown marks, so keep shaking!) Turn heat to medium. Wait for the popping sounds to begin.

4. Keep the lid firmly on to prevent escaping popcorn. There should be a big burst of popping sounds, followed by slower popping. When it slows down, turn off the heat and take the pan off the hot ring.

5. Wait until all the popping has stopped before removing the lid and scooping out the popcorn into a large bowl. You can either eat as it is, wonderfully plain, or add minimal flavouring.

6. For a buttery flavour, melt a few small pieces of butter in a microwave or in a small saucepan and pour over, then stir round to coat. For a slightly salted flavour, sprinkle a little salt very lightly and stir round.

You should find that any unpopped corn kernels drop to the bottom of the bowl. Throw them away. They are far too hard to crunch on!

25

Perfect pink pretzels ∨

Actually, the pink bit is optional, but the perfect part is guaranteed!

If you do want to party with pinkness, all you have to do is add a few drops of natural (not artificial!) red food colouring.

Ingredients

- 4 cups of plain flour
- 1 tablespoon of sugar
- 1 teaspoon of salt
- 3 tablespoons of active yeast
- 1 1/2 cups of warm water
- 1 beaten egg
- 1/2 teaspoon of natural red food colouring (optional)

What you do

1. In a large mixing bowl, dissolve the active yeast in the warm water and stir well. Leave for five minutes.

2. In a medium bowl, mix together the flour, sugar and salt.

3. Add the flour mix to the yeast mix in the large bowl, a little at a time. Stir. While stirring, add the beaten egg (and the food colouring if using). Keep stirring so that everything is really well combined to form a thick dough.

4. Lightly dust your hands with flour to stop them sticking to the dough. Pat the dough into a large ball in the bowl and turn out on to a wipe-clean surface. Knead lightly by folding the ball in half, pressing down, turning the dough and repeating. Do this about 20 times or, until the dough is smooth and bouncy.

5. Form into a thick roll shape and cut into between 15 and 20 pieces.

6. This is the fun bit! Roll each piece into a really long, thin rope-sausage then make whatever shape you fancy. Make sure the ends are joined up and get creative. Have a competition for the most elaborate design.

7. Place carefully on to an oiled baking sheet and bake at 200°C (gas mark 6) for 15-20 minutes. They should be golden or a warm, golden rose if you're partying with pink. Eat hot or cold, (though you'll probably find they smell too good for many of them to even get cold!)

Sausage sleeping bags

This recipe needs puff pastry so I'm going to let you in on our closely-guarded family secret for how to produce perfect puff pastry every time. Visit the freezer section of your local supermarket, locate a packet of frozen, ready-made puff pastry. Purchase and defrost at home. Follow the instructions on the packet!

Ingredients

- I packet of puff pastry, defrosted.
- Cocktail sausages or mini chipolatas
- Milk

What do you call a secret-agent sausage? Licensed to grill!

What you do

1. With a rolling pin, roll out the pastry until it's about 4mm ($1/8$ inch) thick.

2. Cut into rectangles big enough to wrap completely around each sausage so that the sausage will be hidden inside.

3. Use a pastry brush to brush a little milk down one edge of the pastry rectangle. Wrap up the sausage from the other side of the pastry so that you are rolling it over towards the milky edge. This acts like the gummy flap on an envelope and should stick firmly down to keep the sausage rolled up. Put the sausage-filled sleeping bag to snooze on a baking tray. It's best to put it down with the edge of the wrapping underneath so it won't uncurl.

4. Brush the top with a little more milk and repeat until all the little sausages are ready for bed!

5. Bake for 12-15 minutes in a pre-heated oven at 180°C (gas mark 5).

sausages!

The Sausage Game

Play this while munching the sausage sleeping bags.

The object of this game is to answer 20 questions without laughing.

Sounds easy? Not when you can only answer by saying "sausages" to every question. What's your name? What are you wearing on your feet? What do you use to wash your hair? What does your nose look like? What's in your bag?

Layer sandwiches

Have you ever thought that sandwiches look *reeeaaally* boring? These ones don't just sit on the plate, they practically jump up and down, yelling, "Eat ME! Nooo...ME!" Much more exciting and not only are they better-looking, they taste fabulous too. Why stop at four layers? Find out how high you can go!

Ingredients:
- Bread slices
- Margarine or butter
- A variety of fillings to choose from such as grated cheese, cottage cheese, ham, tuna, houmous, cucumber/tomato slices, mayonnaise, lettuce, cress, coleslaw, grated carrot, guacamole, thin salami, pate, tahini or sliced olives

What you do

1. Spread four pieces of bread with butter or margarine.

2. Place an interesting combination of fillings, (say cottage cheese and coleslaw) on to the first slice.

3. Place a second slice of bread over the top to create the first layer.

4. Now butter this top slice and choose another filling (say, lettuce and mayonnaise).

5. Place the third slice of bread over the top for your second completed layer.

6. Repeat the process of buttering and filling (say, cucumber and salami) and top off with the fourth slice.

7. Use a bread knife to carefully slice the mega-sandwich into triangles. When cutting, imagine that you are gently sawing a piece of wood. It really works! Move the knife backwards and forwards, don't press it straight down. That way you won't end up with squidged sandwiches.

Roly poly sandwiches

These are SO easy that they really require no introduction. Spread. Roll up. Stick in a cocktail stick. What are you waiting for?

Ingredients
- Ready sliced bread
- Soft butter or margarine
- Spreadable or thin fillings such as: soft cheese, pate, tuna mayonnaise, grated cheese or thin ham.

What you do

1. Carefully cut off the crusts from each piece of bread.

2. Butter each slice and spread the fillings of your choice.

3. Cut in half lengthways. (Or, cut into four strips if you want really mini mouthfuls).

4. Starting at one end, roll up as though you are rolling up a rug. Then jab a cocktail stick through to keep everything in place. It's a sandwich...in disguise.

5. If you want to be ultra sophisticated, place an olive on the end of the cocktail stick (or small pieces of chopped cucumber or tiny cherry tomatoes). Now it's a sandwich with a handle!

Practical Joke

Here's a horrid trick to play while you've got any carrots out of the fridge.

You will need a pair of gloves and a carrot that is roughly the size of your thumb. Fold your thumb across the palm of your hand, with a carrot gripped in place of where your thumb ought to be. Put on a pair of gloves, with the carrot in the thumb place. Ask your mates if they dare you to "break" your thumb.

Grasp the carrot thumb and snap it. Screech convincingly in agony!!!

What's orange and sounds like a parrot? A carrot!

29

superb suppers

A substantial supper is a key part of the whole sleepover if everyone is to have enough energy to keep going.

Recipes:

- Pasta perfect pasta • Salads • Dinner jackets • Pile-it-in-pitta • Fluffy falafels
- Dazzling dahl with nan bread • Tasty tacos

Pasta perfect pasta V

A hearty bowl of pasta or spaghetti with pasta sauce, topped off with lashings of grated cheese – yum. And so easy too. Make the sauce first so that it's ready to tip straight over the pasta once it's cooked.

Ingredients

- 2-3 tablespoons of olive oil
- 1 onion • 1 clove of garlic
- 1 teaspoon of mixed, dried herbs (or dried basil) • Salt
- 1 tin of chopped tomatoes
- 6 chopped mushrooms, 1/2 chopped red pepper, 2 teaspoons tomato puree (optional), 4 chopped spring onions, fresh chopped basil instead of dried herbs (optional)

What you do

Pasta Sauce

1. Chop the garlic finely or squeeze it in a garlic press. Finely chop the onion (and mushrooms, pepper and spring onions if using).

2. Place a medium-sized saucepan on a medium heat and add the oil. Add the garlic and the onion and a sprinkle of salt and cook slowly while stirring. You want the onion to soften and not go brown, so if it seems to be cooking too quickly, lower the heat. After a couple of minutes, add dried herbs and any other chopped ingredients. Continue to stir. Cook on a low heat for 5-10 minutes until nice and soft.

3. Add the tomatoes (and fresh basil if using). Stir. Cook on a low heat for 20-30 minutes.

4. Remove from the heat and put a lid on to keep it warm.

Pasta

1. Fill 2/3 of the large saucepan with cold water. Add one teaspoon of salt and put on a high heat and bring to the boil.

2. When boiling, turn to a medium heat and pour in the pasta. Stir to prevent sticking and return to the boil by turning back to full heat. Once boiling, keep on the boil by adjusting heat down enough to keep it bubbling. Follow the instructions on the packet for how long the pasta needs to cook for.

3. When you think it is ready, test by removing a piece (or strand) and tasting. It should be firm to the bite but not hard to bite through.

4. Place a colander in the sink and carefully pour the contents of the saucepan into it. Shake all the water out. Return the pasta to the pan and drizzle over a little oil and shake the pan. (This provides more non-stick help.)

!
This may require adult help as it could be very heavy and being rushed to hospital with scalding burns will not make for the best sleepover.

5. Place the pasta or spaghetti in bowls. Dollop pasta sauce in the middle of each serving. Sprinkle over grated cheese or grated parmesan. Add forks and hungry guests.

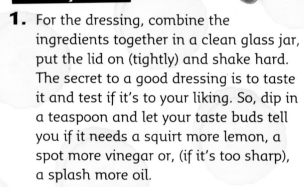

Salads

We'll begin with the humble green salad. Why? Because it's light, refreshing, goes with almost anything AND can be used as the basis for other, more substantial salads.

Ingredients

- Lettuce (1 or more varieties)
- Cucumber
- Any green salad vegetables such as celery, spinach leaves and rocket.
- fresh, green herbs such as either basil or chives (optional)

For the dressing:

- 1/2 a cup of olive oil (or other suitable dressing oil)
- 3-4 teaspoons of balsamic vinegar
- A good squeeze of lemon
- 1/2 a teaspoon of French or wholegrain mustard, a dribble of runny honey and a pinch of salt (optional)

What you do

1. For the dressing, combine the ingredients together in a clean glass jar, put the lid on (tightly) and shake hard. The secret to a good dressing is to taste it and test if it's to your liking. So, dip in a teaspoon and let your taste buds tell you if it needs a squirt more lemon, a spot more vinegar or, (if it's too sharp), a splash more oil.

2. Shred the lettuce and chop any other greenery, using a chopping board and a knife. Put this in a salad bowl.

4. Pour over one or two tablespoons of the salad dressing to begin with and toss the salad. (It just means lifting the salad up and down to get the dressing evenly mixed). If, like me, you like your salad drowning in dressing, add more to taste.

Tuna Pasta Salad and Vegetarian/Vegan Pasta Salad

Add a tin of drained tuna to a pasta salad for Tuna Pasta Salad and for a Vegetarian/Vegan Pasta Salad, add either nuts or seeds or half a tin of drained, ready-to-use chickpeas.

Pasta Salad

To your basic green salad, add cooked and cooled pasta, plus whatever other salady ingredients you fancy.

Greek Salad

Transform from green to Greek with the simple addition of sliced tomatoes, olives and chunks of feta cheese.

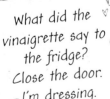

What did the vinaigrette say to the fridge? Close the door. I'm dressing.

Dinner jackets ♥

Plain old baked potatoes will be anything but plain by the time you've finished with them.

Ingredients

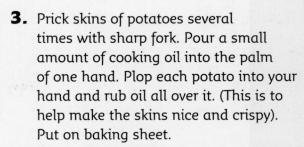

- Baking potatoes (1 per guest)
- Cooking oil
- Butter or margarine
- A range of fillings such as grated cheese, cottage cheese, chopped tomato, chopped chives, tuna, mayonnaise, coleslaw, baked beans and garlic butter
- Salt and black pepper to taste

What you do

1. Preheat the oven by turning it on to a high heat.

2. Scrub the potatoes (if they're not pre-washed) and dry with a kitchen towel.

3. Prick skins of potatoes several times with sharp fork. Pour a small amount of cooking oil into the palm of one hand. Plop each potato into your hand and rub oil all over it. (This is to help make the skins nice and crispy). Put on baking sheet.

4. Bake in the middle of the oven for about one hour (or longer if you're using really big potatoes). They are cooked when you can easily poke a skewer or small knife through each potato.

5. Remove from the oven. Allow to cool a little. Slice in half. Scoop out the middle of each half with a spoon. Put a little butter/margarine in each half so it melts.

6. What you do next is up to you! You can pile the scooped-out potato back in and melt more butter over the top before adding fillings and toppings. Or, in a small bowl, you can mash the scooped-out potato with butter/cheese/chopped tomato or mayonnaise (or other imaginative concoctions) and then pile it back in.

Pile-it-in-Pitta

Couldn't be easier!

1. Purchase one pack of pitta bread (or more if you have a lot of guests).

2. Toast each bread in a toaster or under the grill until very lightly toasted (or warm in oven, according to packet instructions).

3. Carefully slice open one side (like an envelope), peel open and fill with whatever you fancy. Make it up as you go along.

Why did the tomato blush? Because she saw the salad dressing.

Knock knock
Who's there?
Lettuce
Lettuce who?
Lett-uce in and we'll tell you!

These are just a few possible ideas:
- Grilled red pepper (on a baking tray, grill chunks of red pepper drizzled with olive oil, until the pepper skins begin to blacken at the edges) • Goats' cheese or feta chunks
- Basil leaves • Sliced cherry tomatoes • Mayonnaise
- Falafels (see page 35) • Green salad leaves • Sliced cucumber and tomato • Tahini dip (see page 19) or plain yoghurt or crème fraiche • Grated carrot • Coleslaw • Toasted sunflower seeds (see page 25) • Lettuce • Sliced cucumber and tomato
- Grated cheese • Soft cheese • Grilled halloumi cheese • Tuna mayonnaise • Ham • Salami
- Houmous (see page 20)

Fluffy Falafels V ✳

There are very, very many variations on this traditional Middle Eastern dish. This is just one of them! Serve falafels in pitta bread or by themselves – with tahini dip or houmous or plain yoghurt and salad (or you could just eat them by themselves. They are delish!)

Ingredients

- 1 can of chickpeas
- 1 medium-sized onion, finely chopped
- 2 cloves of garlic, peeled and chopped or squeezed in a garlic press
- 1 teaspoon of ground coriander
- 1/2 –1 teaspoon of ground cumin
- 1/2 a teaspoon of salt
- 1/2 a teaspoon of baking powder
- 2 tablespoons of fresh, chopped parsley (you can make it without, but it does taste better with parsley if you have it).
- Oil for frying

What you do

1. Place all ingredients in the processor and whizz (or place in a bowl and use a hand-blender to blend or a fork to mash thoroughly).

2. Use a dessertspoon to scoop out a spoonful of the mixture. This is the messy bit – so get stuck in! Use your hands to roll into a ball and then flatten the ball between the palms of your hands. Put all the squidged falafels on a plate.

3. Heat two tablepoons of oil in a frying pan on a medium heat. Fry the falafels on both sides until crispy-golden. (You may need to top up the frying oil for the next batch as the first ones will soak it up.)

4. Put the cooked ones on paper towels on a big plate.

Best served hot. However, they are also great eaten cold, with dips, as a later (midnight!) snack. This works especially well if you make tiny, bite-size ones.

Dazzling dahl – with nan bread V

Particularly good for warming up a cold night. There are more ways to make this Indian dish than I've had hot suppers. I like this particular version as it's easy, it's cheap and it's made all in one saucepan (and anything that reduces the washing-up is good).

Just a little word of warning on the subject of washing. This recipe uses turmeric – a fabulous deep yellow spice. However, it STAINS.

Ingredients

- 1 onion, finely chopped
- 1 clove of garlic, crushed or finely chopped
- 1 cup of lentils
- 3 cups of water
- 1 tin of chopped tomatoes
- $1/4$ teaspoon of turmeric
- $1/2$ to 1 teaspoon of ground cumin
- $1/2$ to 1 teaspoon of ground coriander
- 1 teaspoon of garam masala (optional)
- 1 potato or sweet potato, chopped into small cubes (optional)
- Butter, ghee or oil for frying

What you do

1. Fry the onion and garlic together on a medium heat for a couple of minutes, stirring lots.

2. Add the cumin, turmeric and coriander. Stir well and continue frying for 3-5 minutes.

3. Add the tin of tomatoes, the cup of lentils and three cups of water (recently boiled water will help speed things up). If you're using potato, add this now too. Turn up the heat and bring to the boil.

4. When boiling, put a lid on the saucepan and turn it down to a low heat to simmer for 20-30 minutes.

5. After the first 10 minutes, add garam masala (optional) and stir. (Check regularly that dahl is not sticking to the bottom of the pan by giving it a good stir.) It's ready when it's gloopy and mushy! Add a sprinkle of salt and stir in.

6. Serve in bowls accompanied by nan bread which you have worked feverishly to prepare beforehand (ie, you have opened a packet of ready-made nan breads and heated them gently in the oven). Personally, I like to add a squeeze of lemon juice into my bowl of dahl, plus a dollop of plain yoghurt.

!
DO try to avoid dropping any dahl down your t-shirt, or, worse, on a light-coloured carpet. You have been warned!

Yum!

Who's Who?

For this game, you'll need post-it notes or pieces of paper and safety pins.

Each person writes down the name of a very famous person (either alive or dead), but doesn't show anyone else. It's important that you choose VERY well known people so that everyone is likely to have heard of them!

Next, stick the names on to each other's backs (without anyone seeing the name being put on their own back, but so everyone else can see). The object of the game is to find out who you are by asking questions. Only 'yes' and 'no' answers are allowed.

Am I an actor?
Am I dead?
Am I a real person?
Do I sing in a band?

AUDREY HEPBURN

Tasty tacos ♥

Another pick 'n' mix, self-serve creation for you and your guests to have fun with. A great Mexican, all-in-one rolled or folded sandwich-blanket.

You'll need a pack of soft, corn tortillas (follow the instructions on the packet for warming).

Choose fillings according to what everyone likes and put each filling into separate bowls. Add them to the middle of your tortilla but leave enough room to roll it up and fold over the bottom (so that all the filling doesn't drop in your lap). Fantastic fillings include shredded lettuce, chopped tomatoes, grated cheese, small pieces of cold chicken, ham, guacamole (see page 21), salsa (see page 20), sour cream or crème fraiche, and warm tinned fried beans.

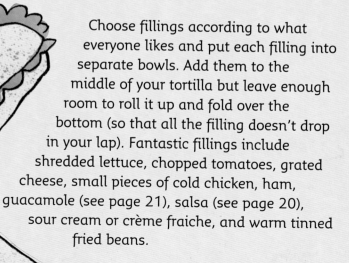

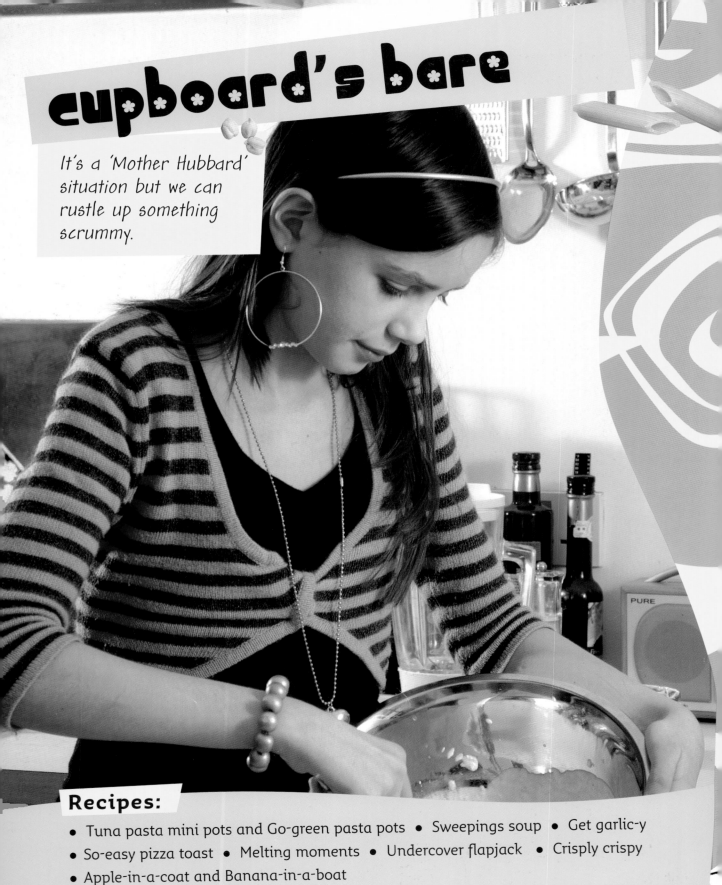

cupboard's bare

It's a 'Mother Hubbard' situation but we can rustle up something scrummy.

Recipes:

- Tuna pasta mini pots and Go-green pasta pots
- Sweepings soup
- Get garlic-y
- So-easy pizza toast
- Melting moments
- Undercover flapjack
- Crisply crispy
- Apple-in-a-coat and Banana-in-a-boat

Tuna pasta mini pots and Go-green pasta pots

If you happen to have small, heat-proof glass or ceramic pots in your kitchen (known as ramekins) then you can make this very easy pasta bake in fun-size, individual portions. However, if not, you can just make it all in one shallow casserole or baking dish and then serve in small dishes.

Ingredients

- Pasta (leftover, recently cooked pasta can also be used if you happen to find any in the fridge)
- Plain yoghurt
- Grated cheese
- A tin of tuna or frozen spinach
- Lemon juice
- Salt
- Fresh or tinned chopped tomatoes (optional)

How does a fish weigh itself? Easy. It uses its own scales!

What you do

1. Cook about half a bag of pasta (if you don't have any that is leftover). Put the cooked pasta in large mixing bowl.

2. If using frozen spinach, follow the instructions on the packet for cooking and add to the pasta in the mixing bowl when cooked.

3. Add the plain yoghurt (at least one small carton, but preferably about 4–5 tablespoons) and the juice of a large lemon and a sprinkle of salt. (Note: if you only have a small quantity of yoghurt, use less pasta or the mix may become too dried out in the oven).

4. If using tuna instead of spinach, add one tin of tuna and mix in. Fresh or tinned chopped tomatoes can also be added and help to make the tuna mix more moist.

5. Mix thoroughly and spoon into ramekins or baking dish.

6. Sprinkle grated cheese over the top and bake in the oven for half an hour at 200°C (gas mark 6).

39

Sweepings soup ∨ ♥

I call this 'sweepings' soup because it really depends on what you can find in your sweep of the kitchen cupboards and fridge. However, there are a few obvious basics such as onion (of any variety, even spring onion), either potato or spaghetti, and a stock cube. Thereafter, it's up to you, your cupboards and your taste buds!

What you do

1. Chop the onion (and if using garlic, squeeze in a garlic press).

2. Place a large saucepan over a medium heat and put in two tablespoons of cooking oil (or butter or margarine). Add the onion (and garlic). Sprinkle over a little salt, stir and cook over a low to medium heat until the onion turns slightly see-through and soft.

3. Chop any other vegetables you are using into small pieces and add to the pan. Stir and cook until they begin to soften.

4. Add water (recently boiled water speeds up the cooking). You need enough water to cover your ingredients and then to fill about 4cm (1½ inches) above the ingredients.

Ingredients

- Onion (any type)
- 1 or 2 stock cubes
- vegetable oil (or butter or margarine)
- Spaghetti or a large potato (or several small potatoes)
- Anything tasty in your kitchen cupboards such as garlic, tinned tomatoes, tinned beans (but not baked beans), mushrooms, courgettes/squash, carrots, green beans, pepper, leeks, parsnip, frozen peas, spring cabbage, red or brown lentils (a handful) and lemon juice.

5. Crumble in a stock cube when the liquid is hot. Add in tinned tomatoes if using. This is also the point at which you can add other optional ingredients such as a tin of beans or a handful of lentils. If using a potato, chop it very small and throw it in.

6. Bring the soup to the boil then reduce the heat and simmer for about 30 minutes until the soup thickens. If using spaghetti, break the strands into small pieces and drop them into the pot when it has been simmering for 10 minutes.

7. You can either serve with all the chunky bits bobbing about or you can whizz with a hand-held blender to make a smooth soup. I like to add lemon juice just before serving.

Get garlic-y V

This variation on garlic bread doesn't need to be made in the oven but it does need a grill.

Ingredients

- Any type of bread, ready sliced or cut into slices.
- Garlic cloves
- Soft butter (not straight from the fridge) or margarine

What you do

1. Toast one side of the bread under a grill. Pull out the grill pan and rest it on a heat-proof surface.

2. Place one or two cloves of crushed garlic into a bowl. Add as much soft butter or margarine as you think you will need to spread over all the pieces of toast you have. Use a fork to mash the garlic in with the butter/margarine. Spread on to the untoasted sides of bread and return to the grill until golden and toasted.

3. Cut into teeny triangles and arrange artfully on a plate. This also goes really nicely with Sweepings Soup (see page 40).

What's the difference between a pizza and a game of cards with your baby brother or sister? The first is cheesy to eat and the second is easy to cheat.

So-easy pizza toast V

Called 'So-easy' because, well, it is!

Ingredients

- Bread slices
- A jar of pasta sauce
- Grated cheese
- Whatever else you can find that you may want to put on your pizza-toast such as salami, ham slivers, sliced pepper and olives (optional)

What you do

1. Toast one side of the bread under a grill then remove the grill pan and rest it on a heat-proof surface.

2. Turn over the toast. Spread pasta sauce on to each untoasted side.

3. Add any other toppings at this point, depending on what you've been able to root out. Sprinkle over grated cheese and pop back under the grill until the cheese is bubbling and golden. This is better eaten as soon as it's ready as it turns a little soggy if saved until later.

cupboard's bare

Flour Face

You need a medium-sized mixing basin, a large plate, flour and a piece of chocolate.

Fill the bowl with flour and pat it well down. You are making a flour sandcastle, so think 'beach' here. Place the plate over the top of the bowl. Hold the bowl with one hand and the plate with the other and flip over the plate so that the bowl is sitting upside down on the plate. Carefully remove the bowl to reveal the perfect flour-bowl castle (and if it isn't quite right you can simply try it again). Place a piece of chocolate on top.

Take it in turns to slice portions of flour off the shape with a cake knife. The aim is to avoid dislodging the piece of chocolate. Whoever does finally cause the chocolate to collapse has to pick it up... with their teeth. Flour face! Where's that camera?

Melting moments V

My mum used to make these biscuits with her mum. She said they were called melting moments because they only took a moment to melt in the mouth before you wanted another one. You'll understand once you've made them. A whole plate of these will melt away in seconds before your very eyes!

Ingredients

- 100g (3¹/₂oz) of soft butter or margarine
- 75g (2¹/₂oz) of caster sugar • 1 egg
- 125g (4¹/₂oz) of self-raising flour
- 1 teaspoon of vanilla essence
- porridge oats or slightly crushed cornflakes

What you do

1. Put the butter or margarine and the sugar into a mixing bowl and cream them together with a wooden spoon or with an electric whisk until very well mixed.

2. Beat the egg in a separate bowl with a fork then add it to the butter/sugar mix. Add one teaspoon of vanilla essence and mix together until the egg is all mixed in.

3. Gradually add the flour, a little at a time and keep mixing until you've got a sticky dough in the bowl.

4. In a dessert bowl, pour a layer of either rolled oats or lightly crushed cornflakes.

5. Sticky fingers time! Wet your hands with cold water. Scoop out a large, teaspoon-sized amount of dough and form it into a small ball. Dip it into the oats/cornflakes to coat it, then press lightly between the palms of your hands to flatten slightly. Repeat this process for each cookie, especially wetting your hands.

6. Place the cookies on an oiled baking sheet. Leave plenty of space between them as they will spread as they cook. Bake at 180°C for 20 minutes.

Undercover flapjack ⅴ ♥

This flapjack is undercover because, depending on what you can find, there are lots of flapjack disguises for the basic recipe to wear to give it a different identity.

Ingredients

- 100g (3¹/₂oz) of butter or margarine (or a mix of both)
- 80g (3oz) of soft, brown sugar
- 1-2 tablespoons of golden syrup or honey
- 200g (7oz) of rolled oats
- Whatever you find in the cupboard or fruit bowl such as 1 banana (plus an extra 25-50g (1-1¹/₂oz) of oats) or dried cranberries or chopped apricots or chopped, fresh strawberries or 50-100g (1¹/₂-2¹/₂oz) of dark chocolate, chopped into small pieces, or 1 tablespoon of cocoa powder (use 2 tablespoons of golden syrup in the recipe if adding cocoa powder).
- Finely chopped nuts

For a subtle banana flavour, add a large mashed banana at the same time as the oats. You can also add more oats (up to 50g). Add them slowly so that the mixture doesn't become too dry.

For a chocolate twist, either add between 50-100g chopped dark chocolate after you have stirred in the oats or add one tablespoon of cocoa powder at the same time as the golden syrup and use two (rather than one) tablespoons of syrup in the recipe.

What you do

1. Put the butter/margarine and golden syrup (or honey) into a saucepan and melt together over a medium heat, stirring all the time so it doesn't stick to the bottom. (One tablespoon of syrup or honey will make a softer, more flaky mixture. Two tablespoons will make it stickier with more of a crunchy bite.)

2. When it has all melted and the sugar has dissolved, remove from the heat and gradually stir in the oats.

3. Tip the mix into a well-greased, shallow baking tin and press it down firmly with the back of a large, metal spoon.

4. Bake at 180°C (gas mark 4) for 25 minutes (or until golden brown). Remove carefully with oven gloves and place on a heat-proof surface. With a knife, mark the flapjack into squares while still hot (but be careful not to scratch the tin if it's non-stick).

When cool, turn the flapjack out of the tin and cut into pieces.

Why can't you get any honey in Boston? Because there's only one "b" in Boston.

For fruity flavours, you can add either strawberries or finely chopped, dried apricots or cranberries after the oats. A good handful should do the trick.

cupboard's bare

43

Crisply crispy V ♥

(Or, how to make one bar of chocolate go much further...)

Packet of crunchy cereal such as cornflakes or rice crispies? A precious chocolate bar? Butter or margarine? You will go to the ball!

Ingredients
- 200g (7oz) of chocolate
- 1 tablespoon of butter
- 1 dessertspoon of golden syrup
- 80-90g (3-3½oz) cornflakes or crisp rice cereal
- Raisins, dried coconut and chopped nuts (optional)

What you do

1. Melt broken chocolate pieces, butter and golden syrup together in a bowl. (Either use a microwave or rest the bowl over a pan of boiling water, placed over a medium heat. Stir until melted together.)

2. Use oven gloves to transfer the bowl to a heat-proof surface and stir in the cornflakes or rice cereal plus any other ingredients until well coated with the choccy mix.

3. Scoop out a dessertspoon-sized amount of mix and drop into a cup-cake case (or muffin tray). Repeat until the mix is all used up. The next bit is the hardest of all! Place in the fridge to chill and harden. Oh – the agony of waiting... Remove as soon as it has set and devour.

Moooo

Quack!

You're Bagged! The Sleeping Bag Game

Lay out everyone's sleeping bags on the floor. Nominate someone to be the detective. That person leaves the room while the others climb inside a sleeping bag so they can't be seen. The detective enters and has to guess who is inside each bag by asking each in turn to make an animal noise.

Take it in turns to be the detective and make a different animal sound each time you play.

What is a polar explorer's favourite breakfast? Snow flakes.

Apple-in-a-coat and Banana-in-a-boat V V

So have you explored the fruit bowl? Apples? Bananas? You could eat them just as they are or you could bake them. Got any sugar (preferably brown but white will do)? Any raisins or dried apricots? What about in the fridge? A dribble of cream? Some natural yoghurt? No. How about the cupboard – any lurking tins or cartons of custard? See what you can find and then get going.

Apple-in-a-coat

You've probably got the idea already: fruit baked with its clothes on. Cooking apples are traditionally used for baking but you can use eating apples too. These will benefit from a dribble of lemon juice to spruce up the flavour. You will also need dried fruit for this recipe.

The apples need to be cored. If you have an apple corer then this is fairly simple, as you push the corer all the way down the centre of the apple, twist and pull out the whole apple core.

! If you don't have a corer, ask an adult to remove the core with a sharp knife.

1. Place apples in a greased baking tin or dish.

2. In a bowl, mix raisins or other chopped, dried fruit with a little soft butter or margarine and a sprinkle of brown sugar. If using raisins you can also add a teaspoon of cinnamon powder and if you're using eating apples you can add a squeeze of lemon juice.

3. You need enough dried fruit to fill the empty cores. Then, push the mix down to fill up the middle of each apple and top off with a little chunk of butter and another sprinkle of brown sugar.

Bake for 30 minutes at 180°C (gas mark 4).

Serve as before, by themselves or with other fridge/freezer/cupboard findings.

Banana-in-a-boat

Take as many bananas as there are people to eat them.

Do absolutely nothing to them. Do not peel. But DO put them on a baking tray and bake in the oven at 180°C (gas mark 4) for about 30 minutes.

Remove from the oven with oven gloves when the skins have turned black (they may also have split their skins).

Cut the skins lengthways to open up your banana boats and serve in their skins. Enjoy scooping out the boats just by themselves or you can add a sprinkle of sugar and a dab of cream, ice-cream, yoghurt or custard (dairy or soya).

sweet treats

Sugar and spice and all things nice.

Recipes:

- Chocolate truffles • Fabby dabby fudge • Chocolate dippers • Chilled chocolate munch • Gingerbread art gallery • Teeny-tiny, sponge-light lemon heavens • Chocolate dribble • Raspberry puddle

Chocolate truffles ∨ ♥

Yum, yum, yum. More chocolate. I'm in paradise.

Ingredients

- 200g (7oz) of chocolate
- 100ml (½ cup) of cream
- 1 vanilla pod or 1 teaspoon of vanilla essence
- 30g (1oz) of butter
- 5 tablespoons of cocoa powder

What to do

1. Break the chocolate into small pieces and melt in the microwave or in a basin set over a small pan of boiling water.

2. Either use the vanilla essence, or split the vanilla pod, scrape out the seeds with a small teaspoon and put them in a small saucepan with the cream. Heat the cream until it is boiling.

3. Melt the butter in a pan.

4. Mix the boiled cream and vanilla with the melted chocolate. Add the butter and stir with a wooden spoon.

5. Leave the mixture in the fridge until it has thickened and is chilled.

6. Stir in the cocoa powder and use clean hands to form the mixture into little balls.

7. Finally, roll the balls in cocoa powder and arrange artfully on a plate. Voila! Truffles. Now you see them, now you...*mmmf, yumf, mmm*...don't!

Banana Balm

This is lovely and gooey and leaves skin feeling baby-soft. If you've got any ground nutmeg, then it acts as an antiseptic for a squeaky-clean feeling. The recipe calls for ground oats (they are extra fine). However, you can use ordinary oats - it will just be more lumpy!

You will need

- 1 medium banana
- 2 tablespoons of ground oats
- ½ a teaspoon of ground nutmeg
- Milk or plain yoghurt (or oat milk for vegans or lactose-intolerant guests)

1. Mash the banana, oats and nutmeg together.
2. Add either milk or yoghurt, a little at a time, until the mix looks gloopy enough to stick to your face. (Don't add too much or it will slide straight off and drip down your front).
3. Leave on for 10-15 minutes.

sweet treats

Knock, knock!
Who's there?
Arthur
Arthur who?
Arthur any chocolate truffles left?

47

Fabby dabby fudge ♥♥

You already know that sweet treats are fantabulous. Well, this is the queen of treats.

Ingredients

- 2 cups of sugar
- $1/2$ cup of cocoa
- 1 cup of milk
- $1/2$ cup of butter
- $1/4$ teaspoon of salt
- 2 teaspoons of vanilla essence
- 1 cup of chopped nuts (optional)

What you do

1. Mix the sugar, cocoa, salt, milk and vanilla essence together in a microwaveable bowl until it has a grainy texture. Then place the butter in the centre.

2. Microwave the mixture for two minutes on a high heat.

3. Remove and beat well to blend all the ingredients together. If adding nuts, stir in now. Scrape into a greased, shallow tin and allow to cool. Then place it in the freezer for 30 minutes.

4. Take it out of the freezer, divide into squares and serve. Ready to go.

delumptious!

Chocolate dippers ♥♥

Just the word 'chocolate' gets my mouth watering. This recipe is great because, not only is it (kind of) healthy, it is also covered in the most divine food known to humankind – chocolate, of course!

Ingredients

- 1 plain chocolate bar
- Assorted fruit such as strawberries, raspberries, apple pieces, kiwi fruit and banana chunks

What you do

1. Chop up the chocolate and melt it in a microwave or basin over a pan of boiling water.

2. Chop up the bigger fruits and place pieces on cocktail sticks.

3. Dip and roll the fruit in the melted chocolate so it is covered. Place on greaseproof paper on a plate to cool and harden. Enjoy!

Totally Top Tip
If you don't feel like fruit then use marshmallows for a super-sweet treat.

Chilled chocolate munch V

This is also known as fridge cake because it has to be chilled before eating.

This munchy slab of yumtiousness doesn't need any baking, only heating to melt the ingredients together. What a bonus! Looks great, smells great, tastes great. Easy to make. What else do you want?

Ingredients

- 100g-200g ($3^1/2$-$4^1/2$oz) of plain chocolate (the more you put in, the more chocolatey it will taste!)
- 100g ($3^1/2$oz) of butter
- 1 tablespoon of golden syrup
- 200g (7oz) plain biscuits (digestives are ideal and for added over-indulgence, you can use chocolate digestives or you can use 150g (5oz) biscuits and 50g ($1^1/2$oz) of rolled oats)
- Up to 100g of either flaked almonds, shelled pistachio nuts, raisins, chopped and dried apricots, dried blueberries or dried cranberries (optional)

What you do

1. Line a loaf tin or a small, high-sided baking tin with either greaseproof paper or cling film.
2. Break or chop the chocolate into small pieces and put in a saucepan with the butter and golden syrup. Heat this on a low setting to melt it all together and stir. (You can also do this in a bowl in your microwave.)
3. Break the biscuits into small pieces by placing them in a plastic bag and leaning on them with the palms of your hands (because you want pieces as well as crumbs). You can also bash them with a wooden spoon. Add the broken biscuits (and any other ingredients you want to use) to the warm chocolate goo and mix very well so that everything is covered.
4. Scrape the mix into the tin and press down firmly with the back of a wooden spoon.
5. Put the tin in the fridge. It needs to chill and harden for about two hours so that it's ready for late-night snacking. When it's cold, it should be easy to lift or turn out. Peel off the greaseproof paper or cling film and cut into slices and then into mouth-sized chunks.

Small mouth

Medium mouth

Big mouth

FAR too small

Gingerbread art gallery ∨

Do you find it annoying that this sweet treat is usually called 'Gingerbread *Men*'? Unfair! And you don't just have to make people; you can cut gingerbread dough into any shape you like. What about a gingerbread fashion parade instead? Instead of using cookie cutters, you can mark out and cut your own shapes using a knife with a pointed end. Design hats, handbags, shoes, boots, dresses, trousers... Go crazy!

Ingredients
- 100g (3¹/₂oz) of soft butter or margarine
- 75g (3¹/₂oz) of caster or soft brown sugar
- 1 egg
- 3 tablespoons of molasses or 2 tablespoons of golden syrup and 1 tablespoon of molasses or black treacle
- 250g (9oz) of plain flour
- a pinch of salt
- ³/₄ of a level teaspoon of baking soda
- 1 ¹/₂ level teaspoons of ground ginger
- 1 level teaspoon of ground cinnamon
- ¹/₄ teaspoon of ground nutmeg and a ¹/₄ teaspoon of ground cloves (optional)

What you do

1. Put the butter and sugar into a large mixing bowl and beat together with a hand-held electric mixer (or stir really hard with a wooden spoon until your arm feels like it's about to drop off).

2. Add the egg and the molasses (or golden syrup/black treacle) and beat again until nice and sloppy.

3. Add the baking soda and pinch of salt and about half the flour by sifting it into the bowl through a large sieve. (This will make the dough nice and smooth.) Beat it in then gradually sieve in the rest of the flour plus the spices, while beating. You should now have a stiff mixture.

4. Use your hands to roll it around in the bowl to form a big ball of dough. Cut the ball in half and form two smaller balls. Put them in a plastic bag, tie it closed and put it in the fridge.

5. Remove the bag when the dough is thoroughly cold (it will need at least an hour). Roll out the dough one lump at a time until it's about ¹/₂ cm (¹/₄ inch) thick and get cutting.

6. Place your creations on a greased baking sheet and bake at 180°C (gas mark 4) for 10-12 minutes.

7. If you all want to get extra active with the decorating, wait until cool then use squeezy icing to add clothes/patterns/ details – and then eat the artwork (but photograph it first for your scrapbook, see page 9).

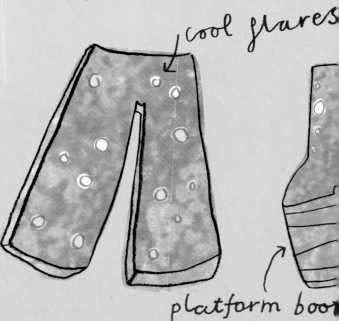

cool flares

platform boot

50

Old T-shirt and Newspaper Catwalk

So you've dreamed of designing? You have wild and wonderful ideas, you want to let your imagination run riot... well, here's your chance!

You will need one old t-shirt per person, sharp scissors, newspapers or old, glossy magazines, sticky tape, safety pins and a few optional extras such as string, bits of ribbon, sequins and glue, felt tip pens, feathers, straws, paperclips or other old clothes to cut up. You can either design for yourself or for each other.

1. Begin with the basic t-shirt. You can leave it as it is, as a blank canvas to pin and stick everything on to OR if it's fairly loose and baggy, you can customize it with a pair of scissors first.

2. Use newspapers or magazines to create a skirt/dress/layered top. Tape together and use safety pins to attach to the t-shirt.

3. Get down to detail – cut fringing into the paper, make paper flowers for decorations or brooches, draw designs over newspaper print with felt pens, glue on sequins, attach ribbon or string straps, make paper hats, bangles, paperclip or safety pin jewellery

4. When everyone is ready, put on music and strut your catwalk stuff! Find someone to film it if you can - these are moments to remember.

handbag

51

Teeny-tiny, sponge-light lemon heavens V

These teensy cakes are simply a version of that easy old fave: fairy cakes. The tiny treat-factor comes from using a pack of paper mini muffin cases. The heavenly-lemon part comes with what you drizzle over while the cakes are still warm.

Ingredients

- 125g (4oz) of soft butter or margarine
- 125g (4oz) of caster sugar
- 2 eggs, beaten
- 1 teaspoon of vanilla essence
- 125g (4oz) self-raising flour
- ½ teaspoon of baking powder
- 2 tablespoons of milk

For the drizzle:

- Juice of 1 large lemon
- 3 tablespoons of caster sugar

What you do

1. Put the soft butter or margarine and sugar in a large mixing bowl and beat together with an electric beater until creamy.

2. Add the beaten eggs, a little at a time, and the vanilla essence and beat together.

3. Use a big sieve to sift in half the flour (sifting puts air into the mix and makes it fluffy and light). Mix it in. Then add the milk and mix in. Finally, sift in the rest of the flour and mix that in too.

4. Use a wet teaspoon to scoop out the cake mix and plop into mini cake cases. Pop these into cup cake tins to help the cases to keep their shape while they bake.

5. Bake at 180°C (gas mark 4) for about 15 minutes, until light golden brown on top. Remove from oven and carefully place the cakes on to a large plate.

6. For the drizzle, squeeze the juice of one big lemon and add three tablespoons of caster sugar. Heat together, either in a heat-proof bowl in the microwave for 30 seconds or in a small saucepan over a medium heat. Stir until the sugar dissolves.

7. Prick the top of the cakes with a skewer or sharp fork and drizzle over the warm lemon syrup a teaspoon at a time. It will sink in to create mouthfuls of spongy-light lemon heaven!

Totally Top Tip
You can make chocolate versions of these too! Instead of making the lemon drizzle, make chocolate dribble (see page 53) and serve by dipping the cakes into a bowl of the warm chocolate – paradise!

Why was the ice-cream and the raspberry sauce left all on their own? Because the banana split.

Chocolate dribble V ♥

There are numerous ways to make chocolate sauce. Serve hot, cold or warm. Dribble it over ice-cream or baked fruit, such as banana-in-a-boat (see page 45). Dip fruit kebabs into it or melting moment cookies (see page 42) or teeny, tiny sponge-light heavens (page 52). There is, thankfully, no end to the ways you can invent to slop on this dribble!

Dribble One:

1. Use half a large bar of dark chocolate. Chop or break into tiny pieces.

2. Pour one small pot of double or whipping cream into a saucepan. Add one level tablespoon of caster sugar. Heat over a medium heat, stirring all the time until small bubbles appear (which means it is near to boiling). Turn off the heat and add the chocolate. Keep stirring so that the chocolate melts and mixes in thoroughly. (If any chocolate lumps remain unmelted, heat again briefly.) *Ready!*

Dribble Two:

1. Use one cup of milk, one heaped tablespoon of caster sugar, one tablespoon of cocoa powder and two tablespoons of unsalted butter. Mix the cocoa with a little of the milk to make a smooth paste.

2. Melt the butter in a saucepan. Remove from heat. Add everything else and stir thoroughly. Return to heat and stir vigorously until it's bubbling. Remove from heat and allow to cool.

yum

Raspberry puddle V ✳ V

This goes particularly well with anything chocolatey and also with lemon flavours. It is stunningly sumptuous poured over ice-cream or sundaes WITH chocolate dribble. What a combination!

1. Use either fresh or frozen raspberries though I prefer making it with frozen. You need about a cup of raspberries. If frozen, allow to defrost. If fresh, add a tablespoon of water.

2. Add up to a level tablespoon of sugar and stir in. I don't add much because I like a sharp raspberry flavour.

3. Heat in a microwave for one minute or in a small saucepan until hot. Stir well so it forms a thick sauce. If you want it more runny, add boiled water slowly until it is thinner and more of a puddle.

4. Taste to check the required sweetness and add a little more sugar if necessary.

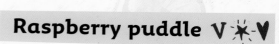

sweet treats

53

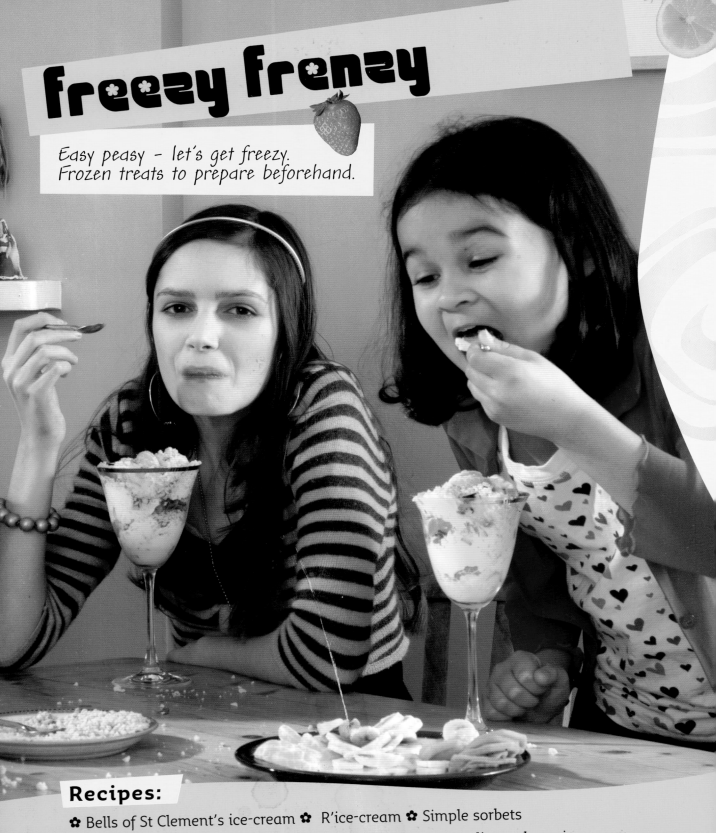

freezy frenzy

Easy peasy – let's get freezy.
Frozen treats to prepare beforehand.

Recipes:

✿ Bells of St Clement's ice-cream ✿ R'ice-cream ✿ Simple sorbets
✿ Ice-cream sundaes ✿ Ice-cream sandwiches ✿ Lickety-split raspberry ice-cream
✿ Fruity lollies ✿ Lemony zing-it

Bells of St Clement's ice-cream V ♥

Oranges and lemons... tang-fastic.

Ingredients

- 2 oranges
- 1 lemon (or for a more lemony flavour, use 2 lemons and 1 orange)
- 1 large pot of double cream
- 150g (5oz) of icing sugar

What you do

1. Grate the zest of one orange and the lemon into a large mixing bowl.

2. Squeeze the juice of the two oranges and the lemon and pour into the bowl.

3. Add the sugar and stir until all the sugar has dissolved.

4. Pour in the cream. Beat everything together with an electric mixer or by hand until it looks like stiff, whipped cream.

5. Scrape into a plastic tub. Put a lid on the tub and freeze until it is solid. (If you make this before 2 pm, you'll be able to eat it by early evening.)

6. If you find it's very hard when it comes straight out of the freezer, leave out for 10 minutes before scooping and serving. Garnish with thin slivers of orange and lemon.

What does a wealthy orange wear at Christmas? Designer cloves

R'ice-cream V ♥

Even if you're not a fan of hot rice pudding – give this frozen version a try.

Ingredients

- 1 tin of creamed rice pudding
- 100g (3½oz) of chopped fruit of your choice (can be either fresh or dried)
- ⅓ of a cup of orange (or other fruit) juice
- 1 cup of whipping cream
- 75g (2½oz) of caster sugar

What you do

1. If using dried fruit, chop then soak in the juice for a couple of hours beforehand.

2. Whip the cream until it has just thickened.

3. Put all ingredients together in a bowl and stir thoroughly.

4. Scrape into a container. Cover with a lid and freeze until it is solid.

5. Remove from the freezer 10 minutes before you want to serve it.

Now, just how easy was that?

Simple sorbets V ☀ ♥

These are so outrageously easy, they hardly deserve to be called recipes!

Simple Sorbet No. 1

Place a tin of peaches or pineapple chunks in the freezer for a minimum of six hours. Then remove the tins, leave out for 30 minutes, open, place in a blender, whizz and serve! *Hey presto!*

Simple Sorbet No. 2

Buy a pack of frozen berries (a mixed bag of raspberries, blueberries, blackberries and strawberries, for example). When you are ready to make your sorbet, pour out two cups of the frozen berries and place in a blender. Add a quarter of a cup of apple juice. Whizz and serve. *Ta Da!*

Feeling fruity sorbet

For lots of possible variations on the method above, try using around four cups of chopped fruit of your choice. Strawberries, kiwi fruit, mango, papaya and fresh apricots all work very well.

What you do

1. Spread out the fruit thinly on to a baking sheet, pour over one or two tablespoons of lemon juice and freeze until it is solid.

2. Place in blender or processor with one cup of orange or other fruit juice and blend until the mixture is smooth. (If your blender puts up a fuss, wait 10 minutes and try again or try in smaller batches.) Add sugar to taste if necessary.

   You can also re-freeze this mix for up to half an hour without needing to blend again.

Why did the ice-cream give up the fight? It knew when it was licked.

Feeling peachy sorbet

Ingredients
- 6 ripe peaches or nectarines
- $\frac{1}{2}$ a cup of chilled apple juice
- 1-2 tablespoons of lemon juice
- Caster (fine granule) sugar to taste

What you do

1. Chop the fruit into chunks and remove the stones. Pour over the lemon juice so the fruit is well covered.

2. Spread about half of the chunks in a well-spaced, single layer on a baking sheet and place in the freezer until it is solid. Place the remaining chunks in a covered bowl in the fridge.

3. Whizz together the frozen and chilled fruit and the chilled apple juice. If needed, sprinkle in a small quantity of caster sugar.

4. You can either eat immediately or return to the freezer for an hour to firm the iciness.

Ice-cream Monday, Tuesday, Wednesday, Thursday, Friday, Saturday sundae ∨ ♥

I like to use at least three different types of ice-cream in a sundae. Shop-bought ice cream is fine but home-made is even more special. There's only ONE way to make sundaes at a sleepover – and that's with your friends!

Ingredients

- Ice-cream
- A variety of toppings and layerings to choose from such as chopped nuts, sliced and chopped fruit, chocolate chips, crushed biscuit and sauces (see page 53 for raspberry puddle and chocolate dribble recipes)

Chocolate blizzard

Love chocolate? This idea is for serious chocolate fans! Layer chocolate ice-cream, chocolate chips, crushed chocolate biscuits and grated chocolate and top off with chocolate dribble sauce (see page 53). Sorry... can't speak any more – mouth too full of chocolate...

Red berry Dracula

Layer raspberry and strawberry ice-cream with red fruits. Top with raspberry puddle (see page 53).

Ice-cream sandwiches ∨

Ah, is there no end to the ways to eat ice-cream? Thankfully, no.

1. Use two thin biscuits or wafers and sandwich a layer of ice-cream in between.
2. Eat quickly. (And not just because they will melt, but because if the adults in the house find out how yumtious these are, they'll confiscate them and have their own feast.)

What you do

1. The most important thing is to have fun being imaginative in your sundae creation. In a tall glass, spoon in alternate layers of different flavours of ice-cream and any of your chosen layers.
2. Decorate artfully when you get to the top and drizzle sauce over if desired.

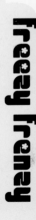

Lickety-split raspberry ice-cream ∨ ♥

Super-quick, licketty-split – this is the cheat's version that you can prepare AND eat within an hour and a half. It just depends on having a pack of ready-frozen raspberries in the freezer.

Ingredients

- 300g (10¹/₂oz) frozen raspberries (around 2/3 of a packet)
- I cup or 225ml (8oz) of double cream
- I level tablespoon of caster (fine granule) or icing sugar (optional)

What you do

1. Place all the ingredients in a blender or processor.

2. Whizz on a slow speed until the cream and fruit are well whipped and look like sloppy ice-cream.

3. Scrape into a plastic container and place in the freezer for around an hour to get a bit more freezy bite into the mix.

4. Serve! (If you really can't wait, you can of course eat it without putting it in the freezer first – just change the name to Raspberry dreamy creamy).

Fruity lollies ∨ ♥

These are so quick, they only take about a minute and a half to make from start to finish. Of course, the time-consuming bit is the three or more hours you have to wait until they're actually frozen!

What you do

1. Use any flavour of fruit juice and pour into lolly moulds.

2. Freeze until it is solid enough for the lolly stick to stay put when you pull hard.

Totally Top Tip

If in a colourful mood and with plenty of time then make stripy lollies with different colours of juice. Just freeze a layer until it is sufficiently frozen to pour in another layer of juice. Three stripes or more looks good. You can also add in small chunks of fruit such as kiwi or strawberry.

Yoghurt lollies

More lollies so simple that they have an IQ of sub-zero! Just follow the recipe for fruity lollies but use fruit yoghurt instead of juice. Combine yoghurt layers with juice layers for something different too.

Soya lollies

Use flavoured soya or rice milk for a dairy-free alternative. Strawberry and chocolate flavours go well together in stripes.

Lemony zing-it V ✳ ♥

Is it a drink? Is it a pudding? It's a pudding for as long as it stays frozen, but if you don't eat it quickly enough, it will meltingly transform back into a drink. Two-for-one deal!

Did you hear the story about the empty lemonade jug? There's nothing in it!

Ingredients

- 3 to 4 lemons • 50g (2oz) of caster (fine granule) sugar
- 1 cup or 225ml (8oz) of cold water

What you do

1. Squeeze the lemons and pour the juice into a plastic tub with a lid.

2. Heat the sugar and water together over a medium heat until it is boiling. Boil for five minutes while stirring. Then turn off the heat and remove.

3. When cool, pour into the plastic container with the lemon juice and stir. Freeze for between one and one-and-a-half hours.

4. Remove from freezer. The mixture should be crystallized but not completely solid and you should be able to stir with a strong fork and mix it all up.

5. To serve, spoon into the lemon halves from the fridge. Easy peasy, lemon squeezy.

6. If you find that the mix has gone completely solid, get a plastic bag and bash the frozen concoction out of its container by upturning it into the bag and banging the underside with a rolling pin. Squeeze the air out of the bag, place on top of a folded towel and bash the contents firmly with the rolling pin until you have a bag of slush.

! Your parents' new work surface is not the best place to do this, (unless you are planning on a life sentence of zero pocket money).

Sleepover Award Ceremony

Draw up a list of award categories for your sleepover. These are just a few ideas to begin with:

- Best pyjamas • Best face pulled while wearing a face pack
- Best individual recipe item (could be gingerbread art gallery (see page 50), perfect pretzels (see page 26), ice-cream sundae (see page 57), layer sandwich (see page 26) • Best catwalk outfit (see page 50) • Best joke • Cutest teddy
- Best clearer-upper • Best giggler

Make certificates for each one and fill in with the winner's name.

Dress in your finest and have an award ceremony, complete with small prizes for each winner. (Everyone should get to win one category each. After all, the limelight is for sharing!)

freaky frenzy

Index of Recipes and Activities